"Reading his poetry has alwa
ed to Florida-a beautiful and
form itself. He is the rarest oi pucts who speaks to social is-
sues and keeps the poetry front-and-center. Following in the
footsteps of Sterling Brown and Kenneth Patchen, McCaskill
creates his own path by walking a trail towards poetic great-
ness."

— C. Scott Satterwhite, Author of
A Punkhouse in the Deep South and *Li Poems.*

"*Where I've Laid My Head* is the benediction of the church ser-
vice where you never knew you could attend. Where you are
invited to come as you are and asked to leave the light on for
the next person as you exit. It is best read while next to the
hearth made deep in the forest, listening to the babbling of
water and drinking rum."

— Marissa McCaskill

"McCaskill's work explores love, identity, and profound loss
set in the backdrop of the nation's oldest city and across the
Florida wilds. Regardless of your environment, if you've ever
been 23 and wished a night could last a lifetime or found yourself in a new place that felt uncannily familiar, you will find
yourself in these pages. If you haven't, consider this a manual."

— Gena Killion

"You ever wanted to feel all the emotions at once? Read this
book. I smiled, I laughed, then cried. Now, it's your turn."

— Brian Stisser

"Charles has a way of embodying emotion in his poetry. He
communicates from his soul. Charles can put into words the
things that I can only feel, and his words will take you on a
journey of emotion if you let them."

— Hannah Stisser

Where I've Laid My Head

Charles McCaskill

Edited by Flor Ana Mireles

1st Edition | 01
Paperback ISBN: 979-8-9890939-3-9

First Published December 2023

For inquiries and bulk orders, please email:
indieearthpublishinghouse@gmail.com

Printed in the United States

1 2 3 4 5 6 7 8 9

Indie Earth Publishing Inc.
| Miami, FL |

INDIE EARTH
PUBLISHING

CHARLES MCCASKILL

WHERE I'VE LAID MY HEAD

Table of Contents

To all the homes I've known

The bridge is over

My mother is a bridge.
She is strength, stretched out on a diagonal.
Evidence that the best women in my family
are made of metal,
elements bonded together specifically
to carry generations on their frame.

She is the enduring distance
between then and now.
The perfect transportation
over all of the things that claw.

When asked of my patience,
my ability to simply be still,
I reply that I am my mother's son—
something she always said to me
but I only understood years later.
Splinters of her metal are embedded in my joints.
They urge me to be strong but flexible,
not fearless of the distance
between myself and solid ground,
but courageous.

She is courage.
The will to be better than your context,
to be stronger than the people
that will weigh
and beat you down.
To be more compassionate.

I am my mother's son
and I wish I was a better one.
I want to be perfect for her.

Where I've Laid My Head

Crack myself open
and show her what I looked like
before the world began to blacken my insides.
Before I withdrew inside myself
and became a wall
rather than the bridge
I fear I will never be.

I'm sure my dream for her
is the same dream she has for me,
the same dream most parents
have for their children.
Perfect happiness.
A life greater than this small gulf town
is capable of providing.
A love in compliment
to all that she has created.

I'm aware it is near sacrilege
to compare her to Christ,
but she has been my salvation.
The path over devils who have
ensnared less fortunate souls.
Streets have trapped many other lives
with statistics of self-fulfilling prophecies
that say I should not be here,
but I am
because of her.

And if life tempers and molds my bones,
through the years,
through the birth and lives of my children,
and they ask me
of my patience,

of my ability to be still,
my answer will be
"I am my mother's son.
She is a bridge
and you will be one too."

Working poem for Brian Stissser

This poem starts
with a quotation
from a Facebook message
from my friend Brian Stisser
"If something goes horribly wrong tomorrow,
Imma need Charles to perform a poem
at my end of life celebration"
sent at 11:37 am
on the day before his surgery.

Brian Stisser comes from
the same place I do,
the same corner of hood and holy
that is Warrington,
where faith and hard work
are born from necessity
and a will to survive.
Where the cadence of Sunday sermons
battle with that of rap and rock
rattling old car frames.
We were created from some of the same dust
God scooped up off the side of Navy
to be resilient but hopeful.
Our friendship is middle school vintage.
Created in happenstance
and degrees of separation
like two kids who meet
only because their lockers are next to each other
or their girlfriends are best friends.
It continued in awkward stages
of growth and stress,

gaming and one-sided drinking,
juvenile humor
and talking through heartbreak.
Until now,
on its own,
a brotherhood.

He is the kind of best friend
people have in sitcoms,
given a pulse
and actual character.
He is flawed but genuine,
stubborn but compassionate,
crass but careful
with those he loves.
He is a manager to a fault,
a bit of an ass sometimes,
a consummate father
before he even met his wife—
and his wife and daughter
are beautiful.
Their happiness is infectious.
Their love,
a living parable,
love and hope and charity given a family.

Brian Stisser is one of the best people
I've had the pleasure,
sometimes frustration,
sometimes completely immature glee,
to know, and
God willing
for all those who feel the same,
I won't have to finish this poem for a long time.

What will I do?

People will tell me that I am overreacting.
That this shouldn't make me as sad
as it obviously is.
That this is only a "see you later" and
not the "goodbye" I will one day make.
But what do they know?
Grandma,
you have been my first love.
The first example of perfect and unconditional
I have ever known.
I can only attempt to model my spirit
after yours,
knowing I will fail
each and every time.

It is the reason we wear crosses.
The purpose behind each pilgrimage.
Not all of us can walk with faith alone.
Not many of us at all
can exist without a piece of God
to hold on to,
to lay hands on,
to be revived by and remember.
What will I do without you here?
Without your presence
leading me down streets my limbs have grown around.
Routes so primal and holy,
each trip has to be a pilgrimage.
It has to be a vestigial part of my brain
that pulls me to the southwest.
With old gospel songs coming

unbidden to my lips
at times when I was sure I forgot
what God feels like.

How will I remember?
The old landmarks are all gone.
The church is so starved
the pews stick out like bare ribs.
Your house,
my first home,
will be sold and flipped
by hands and pockets disrespecting
and ignorant of all the history.
The thousands of Sunday dinners.
The four generations through over sixty years
who called it home.
Even when it is quiet,
when everyone else is asleep
it thrums with life.
It groans and creaks,
trying to find rest with the arthritis settling in its joints.
I swear I can hear John Henry's ghost in the back room.

You are all I will have left.
The first and last piece of God
I can wrap my arms around.
Perfect love in a body that fails you.
It has been torture seeing how unkind time can be.
Watching the spaces between your bones get smaller.
And the ones between memories only grow.

It all betrays the spirit I see staring back at me.
Mortal flesh that doesn't match the fight
of a woman who grips my hand
as if I'm the last person
she ever wants to walk away from.

It is unfair that the body can't mirror the soul.
It would then be easy to answer
when you asked if you were dying.
No.
You are not dying.
You cannot die.

You are all there ever was
and I wish more of your children remembered it.
I wish there were more of us
willing you to stay solid
as full of fight and life
as you always were,
as you always are.
Because I don't know what I am going to do without you.
I need to hold your hand.
I need to see you smile.
I need to know
that God cannot die.

Ms. Josephine and the warring town

I'm sorry I don't come around much anymore.
Warrington doesn't feel like home these days.
This former town
stuck between Pensacola,
Perdido,
and the U.S. Navy.
Eventually it had to assimilate into the city
or be pushed into the waters,
or worse,
across the border into Alabama.

These streets exist only as a boneyard to me.
Evidence of wars none of us had a chance of winning.
I can't go back home.
I can't find it amongst the bones.
In this perversely named place
where new constantly wars with old,
if you hop the wrong fence
or drive too long without intention,
you will end up in someone's graveyard.
What these streets take is taken indeed.
Lots tend to stay empty.
Houses are left to mimic memorials
marking what used to be.

There is only a cosmetic similarity
between what I see before me
and the memories that have shaped my DNA.
Walking a couple of blocks
because the cab won't come down your dead end road.
Elder Hogan's sermons,
preaching the fire into any given summer Sunday.
Bill's Fine Foods and the best burgers

this side of the waters.

The roads have the same names
but where they end up has changed.
My orientation is all off.

When you missed seeing grandma
for the last time,
I didn't want to stop you from running off.
I wanted to run too.
Past the vacant houses
and dwindling churches.
Past the gravestones
that look like sanctuary.
I wanted to find a place
where no one knew my name
or expected a damn thing from me.
Alabama,
the ocean,
anywhere
but here.

I still do.

We're supposed to say:
"She's in a better place."
"She lived a long life and is with God now."

But God,
when I can't sleep,
when I swear I hear her voice
just at the corner
of my left shoulder,
I would give anything to

turn my mind off,
get in a car
and follow my veins
down that dead end road
and know,
without knocking on her door,
without even stopping the car,
just know,
I could go home.

Translation

What is the translation for
"I don't know you,
but I want to know everything about you"?

What's a friendship that begins backwards?
That starts with a connection
and then fills in the gaps
with likes and dislikes,
current love and past heartbreak?

There is a name for this,
but I'm not sure if naming it
would make it more or less special,
more or less grounded in reality.

I'm not a curious man.
I don't ask questions.
I don't wonder about information
I do not have.
But you are different.
I find myself wondering
about every step that has brought you here.
As I listen,
and I understand,
and appreciate this friendship even more.

And I want to do the same.
Retell all my stories to someone I trust
more than 2 months should allow.
Half-confession.
Half-friendship.

Half a random urge
for you to see who I am.
I can't align our lives—
the cracks in our foundations,
the inner workings of our minds perfectly.
We are far too different for that.
It would be boring if I could.
Planet Fitness the differences.
We won't fit like puzzle pieces.
We won't organically
just mesh like old friends
finding themselves in reverse
all the time.

But when we do,
when there is no such thing
as inappropriate jokes,
when the happiness for your growing family
is contagious.
for someone I basically just met.
When two air signs meet
and just accept
that the winds brought them together for a reason.
When I look at you
and feel this person needs to be in my life,
however that can happen,
that is enough.

The only way back is through

Her lips and hips
are from times
when we used to dance and sing
our ghosts back into life.

I want to grab her by them
and promise her
our ancestors don't damn us
for the sins we commit
in their name;
they revel.

The sap snaps back to life
and flows
as far as the leaves can reach,
as deep as the dirt allows.

Like me,
ravenous and unsure.
Like me,
not knowing what I want
and wanting it all.
Like me,
I imagine.

I want to weaponize words
in ways of warfare
I'm sure we've outlawed.
Whisper her steps wavering
between love

and the place love should be.
Life is for the lively.
This violence
not for the silent.

Tonight,
let the roots envy the limbs.
Let the old souls seek new homes.
Let my reawakened bones
revive new ghosts.

How to love a lioness

<u>Step 1</u>
Love will be nearly identical to war at times.
Sharpen your teeth
and prepare your body for the feast.

<u>Step 2</u>
Your mouth will grow bloody
and numb
from biting your tongue
as she wages sleeping wars.
Hold her.
Some battles are not yours to fight,
and when they are,
weapons softer than claws
are often called for.

<u>Step 3</u>
Roam.
She is a hunter
and these streets,
these pages,
the letters that make up her very name,
are all too small for her.

<u>Step 4</u>
She will cup your face
between two small hands
and call you beautiful.
Call her foolish
and drink her in
in return.

Step 5

You will grow territorial.
You will wear her mouth
along your arms.
Your lips will form her name
as honestly as a prayer.
You will find the perfection of her body
in dark places.
Clouds obscuring the moon.
Kissing trails of smoke
from twin cigarettes.

Step 6

Her hands will probe your bones.
Her jaws will crack into your spine
and steel your back.
Your marrow will become molten honey.
You will be changed.

Step 7

Don't count the days.
Don't wonder about the paths
that have brought you here.
Just enjoy her affections,
tasting of sunlight,
feverish in their hunger.

Return to Sender: A request for my next life

When my soul grows up,
just let me be
Scott Satterwhite.

Afropunk: Sensations I can't forget

It smells like
the closest thing to bliss
a pocketful of singles can get you:
Newport cigarette ash,
PBR
and Hennesy.

It smells like
bad weed and bad neighborhoods
when the worst of both
is still better than theirs
because it's ours.

It looks like zines
crafted for three quarters
and sold for four.

It looks like black skin
in blacker leather
dancing to even blacker music.
Burlesque dancers
performing to lyrics praising bodies
of alabaster skin
while wielding ebony.

It sounds like
two completely different languages
with bombastic vocals,
sky-high fists in defiance
saying "fuck the system."

It sounds like
a young black woman

finding her voice
in the middle of a Ramones record.
A kid from Warrington
crafting his rebellion to the tunes
of the entire *Against Me!* discography.

It feels like writing this poem
vibing to a scrawny white guy
putting his own spin on the genre that raised me.

It sounds like a crowd of punks
staring down police lights
in the wake of the murder of Victor Steen
or yelling out at traffic
at the base of the Chappie James Bridge.

It sounds like Nik Flagstar
screaming out his white privilege
to make space for those in the scene outside of it.

It looks like creating room
when there is none.
By writing it.
By screaming it.
By demanding it.
By taking it.

It looks like history
that not only has a pulse
but is unafraid to bleed.

Hel(l) is where we go when we don't die in battle

If I could brawl
either of our family trees
back into whole
and unyielding life.

If I could splinter bone
(again)
and crack flesh
for something nobler
than a short fuse
wasted on a dense light pole.

If.

But we are here now,
too far removed from our roots
to try to replant into scarred soil.
The battle we wish to win is over.
The soldiers have gone on without us
But their fight remains alive.

In our will to push through the dark,
we make a map out of our pain.
When the trenches won't hold us,
we trudge through the lines in our skin.
When the way back looks more comforting
than the way through,
we push on.
A fighting death
is a death worth living for.

Like your father,
Navy-hardened iron

embedded in his chest.
Saltwater and sea foam
thickening his skin.

Like my grandmother
steadfast and faithful,
molten in her belief
until the very end.

Like your mother,
dragonforce and too stubborn
to go quietly into that dark night.

Like us.

We fight for another chance to say
"not today."
For another opportunity
to argue against
statistic and probability.
For another route
to lose ourselves in pain for a moment
before navigating through it.

One more day on solid ground.
One more line of poetry.
One more beautiful piece of art.
One more unconscious laugh.
One more leap of faith.
One more mile to conquer.
One more fight to win.

Hel(l) is where we go
when we don't die in battle.
God(s) willing,
even friendly fire will be enough
to save us.

We were teenage anarchists

I was a teenage anarchist
when I first re-met you.
In the days of knocking back
cigarette ash and sunshine.
In the summers of the waves coming in
in perfect synchronicity with punk rock.
Looking back on it now,
I swear I could hear a dramatic,
"huh!"
with each crash.

You taught me what it felt like
to want to rebel.
Birthed in me this desire
for hole-in-the-wall bars
and mapping out my life's trajectory
based on leaving this planet
a little better off
than how I found it.

Even in the chaos of it all,
I don't know if I will ever
fully appreciate those days
like I should.
Comradery before I would even think
to call someone a comrade.

I could see years over the horizon
arguing about the gears in machinery
neither of us could actually fix,
over cheap weed
or cheap beer.

I could see what would happen
as if I was looking in a mirror
because I was.

There is a feeling that is both
joy and sorrow.
For a moment in time
our lives existed,
in not parallel,
but close.

Life happens.
Choices happen.
I won't ever grieve your joy.
Your life of love and purpose and family.
Even from afar,
even looking at a mirror,
where the reflection has changed,
I wish and hope
and pray
you well.

Indelibly stained
in reflective glass
circa 2006 et. al.
is happiness for your happiness.

The heart is a large
contradicting thing.
It holds memories of versions of ourselves
caught on the corners
of one of our valves.
Emboldening in us
a need to riot

and throw bricks
and fight the power
and yell
when the waves of our blood
crash
the right way.
Hit the right aches.

There is also sorrow
that the future that I saw so clearly
I'll never see again.

Conversation with Ms. Josephine

They think I'm crazy
'cause I come out here
and just walk and cry.
They ask me,
"Ms. Josephine, where you walkin'?
Ms. Josephine, why you cryin'?"
I tell 'em, I don't know.
But I do.
I gotta cry.
I gotta let this pain out or Im'a die.

I hear 'em sometimes.
I swear 'fo God I do.
Ms. Lelia and Bo.
It be so real sometimes
I have to stop myself from talkin' to them.
I can't tell that to my doctor.
God knows I can't.

I'm not crazy.
I just miss 'em.
I'm just old.
That time be weighin' me down.
And don't nobody around here know.
They don't know nothin' bout it.
All these young people here.

Everybody done gone and died.
I'll be callin' someone I used to talk to.
And they pick up the phone
and tell me they died.

They tell me that they been dead.
What am I supposed to do now?
She was my best friend.
She was like a momma to me.
These people see me cryin'.
Just sitting out here cryin'.
But they don't know.

I remember everythin'.
That time weighs me down.
What am I supposed to do?
I don't know what to do.
But just wait for my time.

You tell your mom to come see me.
And bring them babies around.

Eulogist

There's a poem
in the fact that I'm basically
the eulogist of my family now.
There's a poem in that
I carry on my grandma's tradition
of holding on to funeral programs,
this collection
of "preceded by" and
"survived by"
that makes for a truly
sorrowful way
to construct a family tree.

There is a poem
in that I hold on to this death,
embrace and honor and remake it,
but won't have children
and create life
to add to that tree.

For Timmy Boy

When we lose someone here,
we always mention
how they aren't in anymore pain.
This life
and this body
can end,
so can hurt.
But when we go Home
we aren't in pain
OR
time.

There is no need
to worry about tomorrow
when the sun never meets the horizon.
There is no reason
to hurry or speed
when you have already arrived.

Time describes moments
that are not now.
But God is now,
is always now.
And you are with Him now.

God will greet you
like you have always been there
because you have.
Always.
You just blinked
and grandma
and all of our family
will see you

in place outside
of pain,
outside of time,
outside of worldly concerns.
This is life
that always was.
This is Home
that never wasn't home.
Just blink
and I'll see you there soon.

For Uncle Dan

Many years ago
a seed was planted,
in a time and place
where it was hard to grow much,
without it being chopped down,
neglected,
lost to the harsh environment.
But it was planted
in a patch of good soil
here in the south.
And it grew,
taking on the names of those
who joined and nurtured
and cared for its growth.
Moorer and Bryant and Williams and on and on.

It grew,
passing down the lessons
of those who gave it roots.
Be kind but strong.
Be faithful and hard working.
Be a family,
even when miles
and days
and overseas tours of duty
and sickness
may interrupt.

It grew,
even without the members
who went on before us.
The tree is still here.
Still standing.

Still growing.
The years
and the weather
and the sometimes unkind life
here on earth
does not stop that.

As we carry the memory
of one of our roots.
As we say goodbye to him
in this life,
knowing we will see him in the next.

As Uncle Dan
transitions
from being a living part of the tree
to being a part of its
foundation,
we will never truly be without.
We will carry his name.
We will hold on to the lessons
he taught us.
We will care for this tree,
this family,
as he did.
As all the others did before.

Six years

This isn't a poem about grief
or maturely processing grief.
In this,
I am wholly selfish.
In this,
an allegory in which I know the moral,
but damn the moral.
I want you back here, Grandma.
Living and loving and breathing.

What kind of monster
does that make me?
To wish you back
into a reality of dementia and frailty?
But even when your mind turned
friends and family
into strangers and adversaries,
you never forgot me.
Never forgot my face.
Never stumbled over my name.
Or mistrusted my help.

It's been six years
and I haven't forgotten you either.

It's been six years
and my world still goes soft around the edges
when at work an elderly black woman asks for help.
I still find whatever defenses I've built up
crumbling all around me
when I see pieces of you
reflected back at me
through wizened eyes

33

or a maternal step.

It's been six years
and I still can't let myself loose
in this mourning
because, like the rains here,
I'm never sure when the waters
will actually stop falling.

It's been six years
and logically I know
you lived a long life.
A near century
is more than a vast majority of us
will ever get.
But I can't help but grieve
the opportunities I wasted.
The nights I could have sat
at the foot of your bed
and asked about
each and every one of your 36,470 days.
The days I could have read you
every one of my poems.

It's been six years
and God willing,
I will spend more days on this earth
without you
than with
and that terrifies me.

It's been six years
and I still remember the last day I saw you.
Your living room perpetually full of love
and acceptance and joy and home.

Now crowded with family
seeing you off to spend
the last of your days in Texas.
I still remember you looking
at no one else but me
as if it pained you
just as much.
I would give anything
to have you look at me like that again.
I would tear open heaven
with my bare hands
to have you look at me like that again.

Look at me!

Please.

It's been six years
and I'm a man now.
A good man.
I have an amazing wife
who you would love.
Who without even meeting you,
helps me keep your memory alive
in my bones,
in the center of our family.
I have friends who love me fiercely.
And I stand in front of groups of people
and speak words
and make them feel accepted.
Make them feel loved.
Make them feel at home.
Like you did.
And it's not in a church
like you thought it would be,
but sometimes it feels that way.

Or maybe that's you.

Maybe this is enough.
By doing this,
unburdening my grief
in front of poets
unburdening their own,
maybe it's enough to,
if not tear open heaven,
then slide a letter under a door.

It's been six years.
I hope these lines find you well.

Busy Bee Mercantile

This scares them.
This right here
is terrifying to them.
A million
or a thousand
or a dozen people
gathering in the communal beauty of
"for us, by us."

They outlaw, including us,
and are shocked when
our inclusion is bombastic
and unapologetic.

They pathologize our love and beauty
and don't understand
when we deify the face in the mirror
or the love that draws joyous laughter
and tears of gratitude from that face.

We were held by the whims
of an economy we couldn't freely participate in
and they are mortified
when we forge a business
that seeks to keep money in the hands of our people
instead of at the expense of them.

But this day isn't about them.
It is about us.
All of us.
It is about seats at a table
that was set for family,
but by Grandma's rules:

anyone who enters the house
with respect and love
always has a place.

It is about the divine
in offering food to the hungry,
medicine to the sick,
community to the lonely,
counsel to the distressed.

This day and every day you shop here
is about community.
Explicitly inclusive.
Bravely defiant.
Beautifully resilient.
Ever-resourceful.
Compassionate in a world
that doesn't hold kindness in high regard.

And this courageous woman,
who draws the collected admiration
of so many different kinds of people,
is like a tonic made from various ingredients
mixed together to bring balance.
To a body
or a block
or a city.

Beginning again

My walls have unlearned me,
the feeling of being coerced out of my skin.
I am hesitant
to recall the past.
I hesitate
to finger through the previous months.

I've collected them here
day by day.
The piles stand taller than I do
and I'm finding it hard
to decide what to keep
and what to discard,
along with the old bruises
and ashes of menthol
and dozens of poems
that I've swept in the corner.

Getting over,
moving on,
getting past,
is so often an exorcism
or a purge,
but I can't.
The relief from each artifact
gone up in flame is temporary at best.

This is no normal ghost story.
The walls are no more haunted
than the cookie-less fortunes,
or my right hand,
or the side of the bed
that doesn't face the wall.

The spirits are hiding in the words,
collections of syllables I avoid speaking
like a children's game
lest the past comes howling at my door,
crawling through my bathroom mirror.

Words that once tasted
like my first wish
when I still believed in the potential of wells and coin.
Words that ended so fast,
shadows are still burned into the ceiling.

So I still my tongue
and forget old habits.
I resign my skeleton back into my skin.
I retrace the old paths,
lining up my bones
along my blood vessels,
bracing my vertebrae back
against my veins,
sorting what pieces to keep
and what to burn,

and I begin again.

Spitting back spirits
I cannot swallow,
I begin again.

The after

It was as if
we shared a mutual madness
that the mundane world had long since forgotten.
The savagery of flesh
drawn to flesh.
She pulled my blood
closer to the surface than anyone else
had any right to,
black men
and blushing
and all that.
And I held onto it for the longest,
pulling the memories
of yesterday,
five fights,
ten cartons of cigarettes,
half a dozen journals
ago,
back into my skin.

I wanted to bury her name
into the crease in my bottom lip,
the bite marks that had
long since faded,
or the false dimple
of the scar I got when I was seven
when I balanced on a basketball
and I wanted to see how many times
I could catch myself before I fell
crashing into the coffee table.

But love doesn't work like that.

We have very little control
over what we hold on to
or on what piece of furniture we land.
And one day in the shower,
running warm water over
that first dinner with her mom,
I could feel it sliding down
that dumb fight about laundry,
seven bottles of wine,
eight silent nights,
three near breakups,
one that actually stuck,
twelve months
ago.
Flowing down,
and down,
and
gone.

Time for some new memories.

You are life

I've seen you hold worlds in the crease of your grin.
I've witnessed you drink back the rebellion
of midnights in our little corner on the west side.
I've been woken up
out of phases I thought were real life
by the way you could always
shake me and make me question everything.
You taught me
how to be unashamed.
How to offer myself laid bare
and not mutter any apology.
I never thanked you for that,
but I am thanking you for that now.
We are not 20-something anymore,
with the hindsight to be able to call
those versions of ourselves
"kids."

You have actual children,
whose smiles
and mother
make me believe
they'll feel more alive
than their peers
for decades.
I want you alive.
Fully alive.
The laughter of the full picture of who you are
bubbling up from your lips
like water that was always there.
It was only searching for a way out.
A soft patch of earth to let flow.
You are the full expression of what this life can offer.   43

Grief and joy.
The starburst of humor in your eyes
and the rebellion to change what we can in this lifetime.
Intelligent mind and petty judgment.
The thought-provoker
and the tongue-stiller.

Wander

Say the word
and let them have this on their own.
Give the signal and I'll throw it all away
for days among the trees with you.
I have no desire for money.
No need for an existence past myself.
When I end,
let my story end with me,
if it allows me a wealth of days
exploring with you.
Let's roam this wilderness
while it's kind enough to let us.
Let's hunt and teach ourselves
to grow ourselves.
Sometimes the need to wander
with only you and the earth
feels more immediate
than food or drink.

Polytheism

The patron saint of untapped potential.

The goddess of my teeth
aching out of their gums.

The totem in the simple line
from neck to lower back.

The avatar reemerging
strange and familiar
each time she opens
her lips,
her limbs,
her heart.

The prophet that cannot be penned to page
so each time I try,
I fail at heresy.

The djinn I keep captured
in no bottle or dusty lamp but with rope.
I tug my way back
and whisper my wishes into her prison.

The spirit of her unbridled laughter
sends me on a new pilgrimage each day,
across seas of skin that part at my bidding,
across lands that resemble hips.
I press my brow to her belly in surrender,
my gaze always to the west
where that mole on her right leg always calls me home.

She is scripture
hidden in scripture,
lost in the first few books of The New Testament.
I hope that words soaked in holy blood
will keep her from the unworthy hands of the non-dis-
ciples.

Because now all my deities
have dimples I could dive into.
Say my name like I was chosen,
fated to be here.
And all my lives after,
resemble my life,
current,
and it's the only way I ever care to worship.

The misclassification of Marissa McCaskill

My love,
you are illustrations outside of the lines,
sets of beliefs and ideals,
fears and dreams,
that make you a fully fleshed-out being.
A person.
Isn't that the idea of all of this?
To be a person?
To love what is pleasurable,
but also sometimes welcome the pain?
To seek out the discomfort
because it is always there
around the corner,
waiting for us in the space
of someone else's design?

My love,
you are perfection,
if for no other reason than
simply being yourself.

The world will become too environmentally and economically unstable to sustain life so I refuse to have children: A love story

I love you in this life.
I've known you in others.
I've found a love in you
that makes me wholly disinterested
in what's to come.
A complete appreciation
of what has already transpired
to lead me to you.
The near-misses that always held us
one coin-flip away
from each other's orbit.

The two-shade loves
that existed before our own.
When that particular sin was punished
with rope and bullet and fire
for all the town to see.

The end feels over the horizon.
Maybe every generation feels that way.
Maybe every generation
has their own version
of this cavernous gap
between what we owe
and what we're owed.
Maybe every Chicken Little
has their own plummeting sky,
with or without
burning Amazon
or boiling Paris.

I love you too much
to take a chance on chance.
Too much to create a life
that will be damned by conversations
we've kept putting off
generation after generation
before they were ever born.
I love you
now.

"Don't you want a piece of you
to live on?"

No.
When I die,
let the people I love
carry my name
on their lips.
When their lips are stilled,
let me go as well.

What happens when a Buddhist
and a Christian fall in love?

They love.
For as long as this life allows.

The three of us

We found each other
in the crevices of the spaces in between.
The gaps in joints created
when growing up together with someone else.
When the shifting plates
of your maturing identity echo in rhythm.
The two of us already had grown
our marrow alongside the other.
Had spent a near-decade
crafting shorthand for conversations.
Bonding our beginnings
in brotherhood.
Making room for a third
when she found in us
a safety from storms.

Like a magic trick,
there were two,
and then, there were three.

When the telling
and retelling
and re-retelling
of stories
creates an almost culture
in its own.

The legend of
"puking in his car and
still having my back."

The ancient story of
"that photo of the three of us

caught between
the kids we weren't anymore
and the adults we weren't yet."

The fable of
"that time she almost punched that girl."

It can feel
like this is how it had always been,
but it wasn't.
It can feel
like this is how it always will be,
but it isn't.

We're adults now
with responsibilities
and new perspectives
of a new decade
that make pieces of our past
feel every bit
the mythic tale
we make them out to be
in each retelling.

But when your bones
set in tandem
with your two best friends,
no matter the number of days between connections,
you'll always be able to fit
right into place again.

Anima: A view of an alternate universe

She reminds me of an amalgamation
of several black femmes
that I know on this side of the universe.
Maybe they know each other on that side.
Maybe she is a wish that all of us have
for black girl magic to flow
freely and truly and without even a thought
of resistance.
Just currents.
Just rivers under seas.

(Maybe wishes too great for this world go there.)

Just water too stubborn and too sure
of its path to worry about
where it will end up,
what it will meet along the way.

(Maybe it's all some cosmic joke.
Be careful what you wish for, it'll come true.
Just not on this plane of existence.)

She is there.
And real.
And that's all I want for her.

Her laughter is a cackle
of rebellious love.
She embraces gratitude in everything
because her grandmother told her
it is in
every
thing.

The molecules in her sweat
as the late August night
clings to her skin.
Each individual sound
she attempts to isolate in her head,
silently thanking the makers
for their company in the dark.
The taste of coffee
on her lips
and the lips who kissed the hands
who harvested the beans
to quench her thirst.

She is real
and existing in the present tense
and so,
everything that passes through her is joy.
Is blessed.
Is a blessing.

She loves in ways
our world hardens out of you.
In wide boundaries
our roles deny you.
With open arm and hand and mouth and table and limb.
She invites to
"sit and rest and love
while we can
because life is beautiful today
and it will be tomorrow
but I don't know if
I will see it."

She turns my way

but she can't see me,
right?

She laughs.
She sees me.
She tells me her name is
Anima.

She invites me to sit with her.
But I can't.
More laughter pushes through her lips
like a river
I wouldn't be too upset to be drowned by.
She says something else
before she's gone again.

"Life is beautiful today.
It will be tomorrow."

I don't know if I will ever
get the chance to sit with her.
But she's real.
And she's beautiful.

My first two books masquerade as an olive branch

It would drive us both crazy
if we thought about the amount
of good
we starved ourselves of
just because we didn't want
to mend a fence or offer an olive branch.

A decade wasted in some attempt
at a silent cease-fire.
So much time.
I only recognize scattered
remnants of who I was
ten years ago.
My name is still the same.
I'm still black.
Still a writer.
Still a geek.
But the way I speak
and love
and fight
and care for my friends,
these things changed so completely.
They have grown.
I have grown.
You have too.

This isn't an apology.
We did all of that.
But dammit,
you're right.

I'm mad too.
The pride of an argument
we had when we were "kids"
that I let silence me.
The many times
I stepped on a poetry stage
or held a mic
and knew
part of the reason I did
was that you believed I could
years before.

The stubborn inaction
of the embodiment of
Newton's first law of motion.
It was far easier
to stay away and still
than work up the nerve
to offer my genuine condolences
after your dad passed.

Wishing I could have had you in my life
when my grandma died.
One of the few people
I shared my corner of Warrington with.

Whatever happened in the past,
we're here now.
The fence is fixed.
The olive branch is there
and in the hands of people
who think they're just holding books.
The bridge was never
burned beyond use.
We no longer have to starve.

The Bryant-Moorer Family Reunion

Before I was anything to anyone
outside of this family.
Before I found the words to create
who I was or would be
as a friend,
as a husband,
as a writer.
Before I knew there was a world
outside of the sounds of hymns
and the rhythm of family telling stories
in the quiet of summer nights.
Before I could think of how big these lives are.
Before I could fathom that my days would stretch on
faster than I could keep track.
Before life just sort of happened.

I was held by this family.
I was kissed and loved
and raised by 100 hearts
before I knew what kind of gift that is.
Before I knew not everyone was so blessed.
Before.
Before,
before.

I was connected to a tradition
of compassion
and humility.
Of giving what you could,
even when the only thing you had to give
was your love and faith.
Before I would go anywhere,

I was born onto roads that only existed
because people, who were gone before me,
loved and worked and survived.

Before anyone would call my name,
my name was miracle.
My name was light.
My name was the sound of laughter erupting in a room.
My name was the squint in eyes
of faces feeling pure joy.
My name was Rose Mary's son.
My name was Mattie Moore's grandson.
My name was Nunar Moore's great grandson.

Before I knew my place in any of this,
a community of family,
of kith and kin,
gave me a warm soft space
to build
me.
There are spaces in my bone marrow,
in my DNA,
that no one but you all
and God
will ever know.
Whatever I am.
Whatever I ever will be.
I owe everyone in this room,
every branch,
every leaf on this tree.
And I take you all with me
in the deepest spaces,
in the very first parts of myself
that ever existed.
I love you all.

Code-switching 'for the devil catches us

I find myself having to focus
to understand what I'm hearing.
The rhythmic timbre
of black voices in joy
and jest.
The playful bounce
of playing with language
and birthing songs,
both new and familial.
How could I not remember?
I was born to this.
My milk-tongue carries
the sweetness of moms
and aunties
turning conversations into hallelujahs
by some accidental miracle
of knowing what you needed to hear
or understanding
what kind of prayer your silence
was searching for.
Yes, the devil is in the details.
And yes, the devil is
in this world with us.
But God, we are alive.
How can we not afford to say our own names
with honey and cinnamon?
How can we not turn any space that will hold us
into Grandma's living room
or the barbershop
or the A.M.E. church
or any haven we can stumble into?
These days are not promised.

There is so much anger
and despair
that these tiny revolts of light
feel like an act of war.
That being able to engage in them
feels shameful sometimes.
In the time I've spent writing this,
four (that I know of)
more unarmed black people were shot
by police.
What am I doing laughing on aisle 5
when I should be marching
to the closest precinct
lighting everything ablaze as I go?
But we are here,
alive
and capable of laughter
even around the sorrow
caught in the back of our throats.
'for the devil brings us back down to earth,
let us live in revolt.

Lib(er)ations

A toast
to brown hands
lifting brown bags
guarding brown bottles
tipping out brown liquid
onto brown dirt
to mourn brown bodies
that will never
drink down
drops of golden sun
again.

A toast to
names spoken
and remembered
as tiny frothing rivers
are created by this
small ritual.
Jerome
and Jonny
and Poot
and Michael
and Omar
and Amanda
and Sherry
and Brenda
and every one
made sacred,
if but for a moment
by someone thinking of them
fondly.

A toast to
those gathered
on corners,
hugging the first few steps
outside the corner liquor store.
Holding community council
or just searching for relief
in this cruel life.

A toast to those
who bear the brunt
of judgements from passing vehicles
while white privileged hands
fork over fistfuls of cash
to live in walking distance
of their favorite bar.

A toast to the sweetness
of grapes and malt,
sugarcane and barley
that finds its way
through earth and lips
to bless your memory.

Estd. 1898

"If you could go back in time
to any place or period,
where would you go?"

I had a dream the other night.
That I existed in a time
in which my friends and family
would be treated with care and respect.
That same night
you had a dream
that you could relive
the glamor of the past.
That you could flourish
in the dignity of quiet and calm
from a time before
when things were great again.

I awoke with a start,
disappointed that your dream
canceled mine out.
Only to realize too late
I was stuck in a fracture of yours.

I roamed the streets.
Frantic and searching for my people.
To tell them.
To warn them.

The sky is falling.
Can't you see?
It's been falling.
The clouds only look stationary

because we've been
conditioned to hold up the heavens.
They brought me back here,
but they can't make me play their damn games.
Can't make me sit idly by
as they toast to the artistic way
red lines make for effective walls.
They can't go back in time
and keep ignoring
what they never acknowledged
their first time around.

Looking for each brown face within my gaze,
call me soothsayer.
Call me madman,
but God,
just listen to me.
Melt down your melanin
into bullet and bullion
cause they're the true currency
of this country
and their markets
will never depreciate us.
I don't know if by telling you this
I'm undoing my own creating,
but I don't care.

Whisper the names
of every ebony body
turned sickly brown
by the short arm
of the unjust universe.
Say their names now.
And always.
Name the stars in the night sky

for Trayvon
and Omar
and Sandra.
These names don't mean anything
right now,
but I promise you,
some day,
a child will look towards the heavens
and know they shine just for him.

Where are you?
I know this used to be a black town.
I know these buildings
used to house black lives.
Before pollution and inebriation.
Before scare tactics
And The Great Migration.
Please just listen to me.
We have to feed the rich
to the poor now.
The seats are gonna fill up soon.
Grab your knife and fork
and napkin too.
'Cause we're still in the south
and table manners still count
more than what's on the actual table.

I don't know how to stop
my present from happening.
I only have one shot at this.
Lives are depending on me.
Don't you get it?

Can't you see?

Where are you?

...

Wait, what year is it?

I never left?

I've been screaming at cars
and into abandoned churches
and hipster bars
with a fistful of
black gold and bullets?

...

What was the question?

"If you could go back in time
to any place or period
where would you go?"

...I wouldn't.

For Gina with an "i"

How dare we want all that is ours?
How dare we want a more perfect union?
A more careful collection of voices?
A more inclusive way to live out loud?
Supremacy and division
crafted this society.
Made unseen foundations
out of our culture.
How dare we want to uproot
the roots that were ours anyway
and place them neatly
back into the hands
that first nurtured them?
Put the beauty
of our dance and rhythms,
our soul and joy and triumph
back into the light of day,
the beauty of a bronze spring
heavy with belonging.
We didn't summon the division,
but what did they think?
We could hold hands
and slowly chant
the earth's axis back into
something resembling justice?
When they were listening to King and Hampton
did the poetry dazzle them too much?
When they read Piñero or Neruda,
did they not understand what was literal?
Did the meter distract them?
Did the beauty of black and brown
bodies crying out

and demanding their due
make them forget?
Did they really think we had forgotten
what was still owed to us?

Unphotographable: A Photo Album

This is a photograph I couldn't take
of a young black boy
joyously showing his grandmother
around the store
while wearing an Equal Justice Initiative hoodie.

This is a child wearing
the altered visibility cloak
that marks him
dangerous
with the emblem that marks him
immortal.

This is a walking mirror.
In another time,
this is me and my grandmother.
In another time,
this is Trayvon and his.

This is another time
and another black child
allowed his time.

*****

This is a photograph
my phone isn't good enough to take
of a near-full moon
over a still lake
as I sit
near this cabin in the woods.

*****

This is a photograph I couldn't take
of a bunch of black kids
riding scooters all over downtown Mobile.
Of hipster transportation
turned vehicles of reckless black joy
when it's needed the most.

*****

This is a photograph I couldn't take
of being able to hire two young black men
while buildings smolder
and police in riot gear patrol.

This is a photograph I couldn't take
of questions I have to ask
and questions I can't legally ask.

This is a photograph I couldn't take
of trying not to grieve
for the disregard of our specific
human resource.

This is a photograph I couldn't take
of the feeling
that is sadness and hope,
an unspoken acknowledgement of loss,
and much needed grace for opportunity.

If these bricks could breathe

I.
I keep pieces of your home
inside of my home.
They remind me of the fallacy
of retroactive respect.
They remember your name
when that is all that is left
to preserve.
They gave you a day
after they denied you a home.

II.
If these bricks could breathe,
could they plead the case
for their existence?
For our history?
If they could be broken up,
would they expose rings
to be counted?
How many years
would be enough?
How many voices crying out
in their stead?

III.
Am I partially to blame?
For being too late to the realization?
Too late to seek
and hold the memories
I now know to be sacred?
Like the words breaking themselves
multiple times over in grief

over my grandmother's lifeless body?
I should have done more.
Should have held her
and gave her every word
I would ever write about her
while she was fully alive to hear.
If these bricks could breathe,
would they breathe for me?
A newcomer.
A novice to what it feels like
to truly have something
worth breathing for.

IV.
There are so many things I want to say.
What do you call a poem
without a proper ending?
What do you call a series of
one-sided conversations?
What do you call an attempt
to fill in those missing pieces
to try to do justice
by someone you never met?
These words are yours now.
With mobility
to take these bricks and your name
wherever my body allows,
I will breathe and speak.

V.
If these bricks could breathe,
they would say your name.
Pour your name into the sky.
Sprinkle soil
and grass,

73

and gravel
with it.
They say your name
and urge our mortal lips,
still tethered to a place,
where soil
and grass
and gravel matter,
to do the same.

We gave you a day,
the man with the sabbath
in his name,
after we denied you a home.
But this is your day.
Your residence
replaced with a city.
These bricks
replaced with
all the bricks in its limits.
All breathing.
All speaking.
On this day,
from Romana
until the streets end,
from 2019 until
years become meaningless,
we will keep you
whole and holy.

Days like these

On days like today,
I don't just miss you,
I truly feel you.
Like a stream of air flowing
in just the right way
to give an inland population
the surprise of salt and breeze.
It's almost been a decade here.
How long has it been for you?

Do you count the times the air shifts
from your distant shore to ours?

Do you count the songs?
One of the main ways you come to me.
When I fold a sheet.
When I shake a hand or hug a stranger.
When I fight my worse demons
to try to give in to my better angels.
"This may be the last time..."
"...a wretch like me..."
"...on the battlefield..."
Like any people feeling in exile
from the very first home they remember,
the songs remind me of
what I've lost and
what I hope to gain again.

Did you see we did it?
We gathered and remembered.
I'm sorry it took so long.
Maybe we are slow learners.
Maybe the shame of the pain

of losing you
kept us apart.
Some guilt in mourning that isolated us.
As if we could have bargained with God
if we had only tried harder.
But we couldn't,
right?
But how do you know?
How do you really,
truly know?

Do you count the hearts that
come back home to you?
The children you never birthed?
Now welcoming them into the world one last time?
Maybe heaven is just a reset button.
One day,
I'll wake up and be in that living room
looking at you again.
Learning to love and hope again.
The scent of bacon and tobacco
and the kind of wood
they don't make homes out of anymore.
I would be okay with that.

I know I owe you so many more poems.
All the things I should have said
but didn't have the courage.
The humility.
The words.
The sense of self.
These aren't even really poems.
They don't come out crafted or polished.
They are narcissistic impulses

to have conversations with you in public.
They are me trying to
force winds to reach somewhere I cannot.
Do you count them?
Please keep counting.

Brawl

There are words that are not mine to say.
There is a battle that is not mine to wage.
The machine of my body
has more or less done what I've wanted it to.
The vices of tobacco and sugar
notwithstanding,
my limbs and my flesh have been kind to me
ever since I stopped being a child
with asthma and acne and low self-esteem.
I am a happy pilot of a 30-year-old shell,
broad shoulders and chest,
large arms,
steady voice and step.

When my shoulders strain
against the burdens of life,
she presses her pulse into my back
and gives me strength.

When my arms can't wrap around
all that I want to encompass,
my family,
my poetry,
my people,
all of my loves,
she connects her small hands into mine
and extends my grasp.

When my voice waivers
and my feet falter,
her legs show me the way.

But our bones do not strictly obey our desires.
Our internal mechanisms are disobedient beasts.

I am not blind.
I know what people think when they see my wife now.
Crutches and a slow step equipped to a bigger body.
Their judgmental gaze won't know that her legs
are threaded with hours of kickboxing.
That her blood carries the DNA of black belts and soldiers.
That her feet have walked hundreds of miles
through dozens of parks and forests and beaches with me.
That her eyes flow rivers at the thought of all that
being locked away behind a skeleton that does not obey her.

She asks me
"What am I now?"
What is a fighter without the ability to move freely?
What is a nature-loving wanderer that is grounded by asphalt?

If I could implant her stumble into mine.
If I could Frankenstein-like take the best of my physical strength
and combine it with the best of her mental.
If I could build a body that listens,
that mirrors the fight of the woman
that stares at me with determination
to never give in to what is easy.

My grandma would hold my large hands
in her frail ones and remark
that they were "prizefighter fists."

I would think the same thing that I do now.
What use is a body built for battle
when I can't use it in the ways that really matter?

It's a mad, mad, mad, love

Is it safe to say that I made this for you
before there was a you to craft for?
That I see kernels
of who you would be for me peppered in my past?
But I can't paint in rose and make myself the hero.
I won't smoke on tobacco and hindsight
like an old noir film.

What I can say
is that I am scattershot.
The breadth of my focus
Is wide and varied
and inconsistent at times.
I crave the weight of your body
but I feel incomplete
without the occasional kiss
shifting in slumber
of 3 a.m. wind on my face.
Your love,
like sanctuary grounds me,
and matures me,
and sharpens the indelicate edges
that help define me.

And yet,
the pull of poetry,
in the cadence of another voice,
the lull of unfamiliar intimacy,
the plurality of who I am
does not alter your hallowed ground.

What I mean to say is this.
I have been sloppy with my words,

careless with my language
and my love,
selfish and unsure
of what to call this
bag of complications and mistakes.

But you,
are the first stroke
and the punctuation.
The beginning and the end.
With no need for translation or edit.

I want to sin in ways that bring down cities:
an erotic novella

What I mean by that
is I want to rid myself
of any care for the outside world.
There are so many facets of this life
that pull me from my residence inside of you,
from my compulsion
to eat parts of your flesh
in ways that still shock me
and will unnerve everyone else reading this.
From rigging your torso up as a sail
and catching the strongest wind
and the swiftest current
away from any other living creature on this earth
with two eyes and a judgmental mouth.

But our neighbors have ears
and our friends have pieces of our heart
and we live in a world of faults
with enough privilege to make us duty-bound to help
and they just killed more black people
this year
and we have nephews and nieces and

and

and that

breath,

that second that divides
ravenous hunger
for your lips

and the first morsel,
being in exile
and being inside,
in that moment,
I am my most selfish.

Live with me in that moment for a while.
Let the end come
and the fires rage and the capitalism
consume itself as it was always prophesied to do.
Let us know nothing but a self consuming desire
of limbs as rafts.
Of bodies that are broken for bread
and healed again by consuming that bread.

I speak to my lover's madness

Every woman I ever loved
waged war between her neurotransmitters.
Battened down her bones
against storms I couldn't
forecast in time to shield them from.
Swallowed the sugar of compliments
to better stomach the medicine
that maybe,
sometimes,
partially,
most days,
what they loved and complimented,
what they cheered and laughed for,
what they fawned over,
what they came running to,
was the madness.
Unequipped with any rosetta stone
resting in my own gray matter,
save for adolescent anger
disguised as sadism.
I've never felt so powerless
than I do wiping tears
I can't quite translate.
Every comforting word feels like a synonym
for "I don't know what to do."
I've never felt at odds
with my own existence.
I've never had to list the reasons why not.
Every prayer is gratitude
for whatever divinity gifted me
with this peace
and a plea to portion some of it away.

Dear love,

Why wouldn't we consent to more love?
Why wouldn't we want to spend
as many of these waking hours as we can
loving and being loved?
When love arrived again,
why wouldn't we want to accept it,
open the doors,
pull back the blinds,
lift the windows
and let the breeze in?

When joy feels like
having to ration your own happiness.
When the horror of random acts of violence
can end my breath as quickly
and dispassionately
as the plucking of a flower.
I kiss your lips and say a prayer.
Each "I love you" is my last will and testament
that your life is full of love
if I don't come back to you.
Each smile I pull from your lips
like my greatest magic trick,
is a hope that another
will hold the weight of that particular star
if I never get to see it again.

My god,
there is no time for jealousy or ego
when I never know
if I will hear your voice lift in the air
with intimate adoration again,

but if there is a god,
let it always lift.
Let your smile always shine.
Let your kisses be plentiful.
Let your laughter be a river
that flows until there is nothing left
to find joy in.
I love you.
Simply and completely.
Past the boundary of our love.
Into the areas of your love for yourself.
Throughout your love of him.

Dear love,
love.

Katie Garrett and Mike Ensley
are still garbage people:
A goodbye letter to Pensacola

What is the opposite of scorched earth tactics?
Is it carefully reeling in my roots
from the dirt that birthed me
so that something can grow here again?
So that my roots can reach solid soil
in a different garden?
My hands are large and not deft.
They fumble with prunings
and farewells.
Restless fingers wanting to write
strange stories
I've yet to imagine.

I've followed the coastline of our state
down like the hands caressing
a lover who is equal parts bitter and sweet.
The world is a large place
and has never been more accessible than it is now,
with the nomad at my side
and no seeds tying us to any land.
But I am a product of the gulf.
The smell of salt water on the air
is every bit of who I am in my bones.
I have built my body
with the sands of broken shells.
I have loved and have been loved
by the gods of hurricanes
and the lived-in silence
of power outages and road closures.

I have gained and lost and regained friends
over the sweet sticky of rum
and mistakes and poetry.

I was a frightened boy
who became familiar with doubt
and the statement of alone.
And I found love.
My God,
I found love.
Here,
there is joy and a shining face
in the middle of a community.
Here,
there is a voice that does not shake
or doubt its timbre or rage.
Here,
there is a newfound bliss
that makes me ache
because that boy never thought he would have that.
Here,
there is light and sunshine
and laughter and words.
Here,
my family became too many to count.
Here,
my victories were accidental and joyous.

But I'm not "here" anymore.
I'm not there.
What is a word for goodbye to a place
that made you?
What is the opposite of scorched earth tactics?

This feeling.

To love a nomad

You have given me a life
more expansive than chasing a fortune
of made up numbers on a ledger.
You have given me this life
that knows a pure appreciation
of what nature gifts us
and what we are undeserving of.
I have never been nomadic.
My wandering before you
has been tiny in its scope.
With you, I have seen waters
that have carved away stone
with sheer persistence and patience.
I have seen life
that still exists without us.
Yes,
the tree does still make a sound
because we need it,
but not the other way around.
I have seen a forest bursting with life
that I had no name for.
My sense of peace had been a handful of things.
Mundane and fleeting totems
I could fit in my palm before they dissipated.
In you,
I've found a serenity
that is centered wherever there is flowing water,
or stone curved up to touch the sky,
or trees reaching across dirt and marsh to grasp
one another.
You've given me this gift of defining my home

by wherever the earth will welcome my wandering
and wherever your heart will welcome my love.

An echo of this

I am restless without
the thrum of 3 a.m.
The designed chaos
to have my bones
clang against another's
and send music out
into the night sky
like light paint.
Like signals to the other
dreamers and madmen,
insomniacs and drunks.
The hollow pang to grab
everything I am
and toss it against
everything I want to be.
And see what resonates.
Find out what rings far
and echoes back
something true.

My Lady

There's a place
that was waiting for me
to help shed my skin,
just as there's a person
that was waiting for me
to tuck her right underneath my chin.
The first of many kisses that feel like
deja vu embracing me.
The first of many smiles
wielded by lips
practiced with a foreign tongue
and a shared understanding.
The first of many words
written in celebration of soft skin
and expressive laughter
that holds nothing back
and invites me to do the same.
The first of many moments
falling in love with abundant curves
and a fit that feels tailor-made.
But limbs don't come
with custom measurements,
and faces don't unlock doors to peace
simply by existing and shining.
But this is real.
The knowledge of it is as certain
as anything can be in this life.
I know the scent of roses and vanilla.
I know a new name for love,
sprinkled on my lips,
waiting to light up the air again.

Microdosing as a coping mechanism

Logically,
I know
these small amounts
are better
for me in the long run.
A fraction
of a sip.
Enough
of a taste
to remind me
of the
description
of a
flavor.
Incremental
amounts
in my
bloodstream,
still below
any
noticeable
threshold.
But damn,
caution
feels like
not feeling
much
these days
and one
hand holds
a portion

I could
choke on
and the other
holds back
that hand,
and
so
it
goes.

Walt Whitman

I run my fingers through her hair
and feel tiny garnets cling to my fingers.
They catch the light of the sun
and burst into a thousand tongues of amber fire,
shining nearly as bright as she does.
They fall to the floor
with tiny twinkles of sound.
The small noisy cascade of sun showers.
I hold her face in my hands
and without thinking,
lick the taste of sweet cream and milk
and rose and the joy of a life spent
welcoming more joy,
from my fingertips.

"Why be only one thing?"
she asks.
"Why not be multitudes?
Why not be a tree,
swaying and stretching and bending
to the force of winds
or the chaos of life?"

She is multitudes.
She presses her hand to my chest
and I feel a call to battle.
A need to have my skin
wear her aggression like an oath.
A call to arms
that makes me look down the line of her body
like mapping strategies to attack
and conserve.

To make mine if only but a night
and a meeting.

She speaks and my ears want to hold every word in.
Want to bottle the beautiful perspective
that our society does its best
to strip from us.
The desire she expresses
of wanting her beauty
defined by things
you can't see in just a still photo.

She is multitudes.
The brash fighter.
The garnet dripping socialite.
The dancer with elegant power
threaded in her thighs.
The southern charm
of honeyed smiles
and boundaries of briar.
She is multitudes and so am I.
My anarchy borne of
James Baldwin and Fred Hampton
wants to play and rebel with her
intersections of academia,
high society, and social activism.
My appreciation for art and beauty
dreams of committing her body to memory,
writing poetry to the accidental meter
of our limbs intertwined together.

My hopes and dreams
stretch out before me,
days with her so numerous
I will get the chance

to love every part of her
with every part of myself.

Rebuilding my joy

Like a ladder,
Replacing rungs of my DNA
like some narcissistic thief.
Like a magic trick
in which I am the magician
and the assistant,
the saw and the box.

I've known how to travel
from sorrow to happiness.
I've known the well-worn paths
to lead out of the muck
of bad days,
of capitalism making crows of us all,
of the grotesque math
of defining my life by simply
the amount of hours until
I am no longer doing something
that does not bring me joy.

I know what I've done before.
The steps I've gripped
like gravity didn't have me stapled to this plane.
The way the pier smells
like waking up from a dream.
The accidental rhythm of getting all greens
going down Brent or 9 Mile.
The laughter of my best friends
rebounding over and over against glasses
filled with nostalgia and whiskey.
The applause of 300 or 3
raining down all around me.

of familiar tucked away in eyes
that have known mine for a decade.

I feel so cut off from my old mantras.
From the lexicon I've known to pull from.
Recreating joy right now
feels like rebuilding a ladder
when the only thing I have
to craft from
is myself.

Anam Cara

We weren't created from the same components.
The shock of recognition, that speared into my chest
the first time I heard you speak,
wasn't because the elements of your voice
echo the elements of mine.
But years or miles or lives or moments ago,
we smashed into each other and left pieces behind.
The very act of us defining ourselves
happened in the elemental dance
of gravity and collision.
Like heavenly bodies
that are on paths too long and cosmic
to be truly measured by men in one lifetime.
We collided at some point,
and telescopes and charts,
science and math,
were passed down over the years,
to document our next collision
because we would meet again.

As if the force kept
knocking us on course towards each other
and never away.
Notes in almanacs warning
to "watch the eastern sky."
What is prophecy
if not science without a large enough scope?

I found you in that special place
where I was first finding myself.
Molten and metamorphic.
Your fiery joy
pressed into my being

and now,
my heart moves with your happiness
many miles away.
The spark of life
shining at the corners of your smile
burned onto my spirit
and now,
after-images of your smile
performing poetry
are with me.
Your poetry changed my topography forever.
Now, your voice is there
peppered into the sediment of my words.
Where you touched my surface,
I put up waypoints to remind myself
of the impact of deep forces,
of wild primordial magics,
of forecasting the sky's chaos
by what it looked and felt like
some random when,
some crater before.
To remember you and the piece of yourself
you left here with me.
To remember the best friend I have
and how that is still an inadequate title
for all of this.

For Lisa Stisser and all those who love and are loved by her

With the faith that holds a family
through miles and hardships,
we love.

With the hearts of fire and light
and joy and stability,
we love.

With the kin of children that weren't born
but welcomed into a home,
we love.

With hearts and faces
and spirits and laughter
shaped by her,
we love.

While safeguarding
her voice in our mind
and her spirit in our heart,
we still love.

While we hold close
and live the lives
she hoped we'd see,
we still love.

While children grow and cherish photos
and stories are retold,
we still love.

While tears shine on our faces
without shame
because even Jesus wept,
we still love.

It is the greatest gift we are given
and give in turn.
It is a light that is still there
in so much darkness.
It is an energy that spreads
faster and further
than that.
It is here on today
and every day we remember
and miss
and love.

Florida man

In some of my dreams,
my shoulders stretch wide enough
to Atlas the heavens into still,
to reach and pluck
the sunset from the west,
the sunrise from the east,
and gift this land its honorific
in perpetually golden light.
This new state around a binary system.
A state of yesterday and tomorrow
existing in messy collaboration
in which I'll always have
what I've always had
and I'll always know
what I'll get soon.

Or maybe bend plates of land
and deep shelves of tectonic movement.
Fold the peninsula back against the panhandle.
Have my worlds merge into a new land.
Dip my foot into a territory
that was and wasn't already here,
already named,
already my home.

Alive, in love

When I imagined this life,
I had dreams of fluid kisses
in degrees of separation.
A gifting of care
between someone I care for
and someone they care for
and me.

I had dreams of flesh
I could bury my laughter in
for safekeeping
because there is too much of it
in her presence
and not enough when I'm faced with the world.
It comes bursting out of my seams,
aching my jaw with the containment.

I had dreams of existing
wholly as myself.
I am artist
and agitator
and sadist
and bard
and lover
and quirk
and spark
and flash
and stone
and river.

She answers
with fierce intelligence
and open lips
and true peace
and a voice that shines somehow
with her own elemental dance
of forging and crafting and wielding warmth
like a pulse of a person.

I had dreams of not knowing
where I wanted to go
but knowing what I wanted to feel.
Here I am.
Here we are.
Feeling alive.
So very,
so completely,
alive.

Relativity

The stars press
into the fabric of space-time
and bring our attention,
our gaze,
to them.

Pull us into the friction of yesterday,
trapped by the horizon of tomorrow.
Time folds when I am with you.

I feel the fabric bunch and gather
to bring us together
when our orbits are elsewhere.

I-75 is a cosmic speck;
the boundaries between our counties
are insignificant barriers
with a high enough perspective.

With a high enough depth.
I could swear that we were always together
or at the very least,
I could fold
inches,
miles,
light years,
into nothing.

Atoms do not touch,
not fully.

There is always
some space left for space,

but damn the laws,
damn the science,
damn a paradox.

Bring me 1,000 tomorrows
today.
Bring me the atoms
that make up your body
and let them dance
in orbit
with the atoms that make up mine.

Cup

I drink from a cup half-full and half-empty.
Nearly saturated with one flavor of love
and missing others.
My dreams are of building bridges
across shores and gulfs.
My hands,
in bouts of insomnia,
reach for my tribe that I've built
of memory and nostalgia.
Of the wrong words
said in the right ways,
or at least to the right ears.
I create a sanctuary
while mourning a sanctuary.

I look for answers
in the sounds of the literal birds
that fortunately outnumber the "snowbirds."
In their insistence to this life,
too used to the comings and goings of people
to be bothered by their presence
or lack thereof.

I look for answers
in the teachings of mindfulness
and the brash
(and really only way)
I know how to express myself.
By saying what I want,
expressing what I feel,
because life is too short,

and my heart is too heavy
to hold these things back.

I look for answers
in the way the words still flow
like shamanism,
like translating another person's spirit,
even when that person
is technically still me.

I look for answers
in the heat of the day,
the proximity to the equator
and the acceptance of sweat on my brow
and disappointment in the lack
of A/C in my old car.

I look for answers
in the way my wife looks at me.
In the love of a family,
two-people strong.
In the medicine of
unconditional love and acceptance.

I look for answers in the tug I feel in my chest,
pulling at me from the northwest
from people who still carry my name fondly
unspoken on their tongue.

Mangroves

There is a poem in the beauty of this place.
This land of in-between
that I now call home.
The blues and greens and browns
that blend in harmony and discord.
Where water meets land
over and over again.
Where salt blends in and colors fresh.
Brine and sediment.
Brackish streaks
and gradients of murky azure.
Deep wells and persistent rain.
Islands of trees
that filter saline and sentinel floodwaters.
Where the population of man
grows exponentially
but still the wilderness knows its name.
Insists on its place here.
Where few guards divide me
from the wilds that claimed so many
who came to colonize and ravage,
and shielded so many others from the same fate.
There is a sanctuary in the marshes
even when it doesn't look like it
to new or untrained eyes.

Civil disobedience in Naples

One of these days,
I'll find the right frequency
of 808 drums,
or Cuban music carried over from Golden Gate,
or Laura Jane Grace's voice
yelling out rage through a split grin,
to sink these yachts into the gulf.
Until then, I'll keep driving
up and down Tamiami
until I get it right.

Yes

Are my arms large enough
to wrap around all that I desire?
Are these hands strong enough
to hold
and press
and pull
and cup
all at the same time?

Are my teeth
skilled,
sharp,
and practiced enough
to place all of this
into skin
that feels like
a place to belong
and a place to play
and a place to war?

I look into her eyes and see
a binary contradiction.
Feel a split
down the seam of my ribcage.

Lightning that shreds sunset skies
into fractures of plasma and heat.
Water that accompanies
quenching stone and ground.
The sweat of a summer night
as the breeze rolls in

carrying ozone and tension
from miles away.

Her large eyes wryly smile at me
and every thought
that is passed back and forth
between my neurons
looking at that smile.
Is this bloody sloppy heart
large enough to be
poet and adversary,
friend and playmate,
and a safe dock in a storm
and a storm in the middle of a safety
anchored to my ribs.

Yes.

I look into her eyes.

Yes.

Bull-pen

The disaster adjacent to natural disasters in 2022
is how much it knocks us back in time.
The amenities we are used to
become unreliable slow things.
I look at the bars of reception on my phone
and feel strings pulled taut
like two kids with tin cans
trying to make words mean more
than just words.
Trying to fashion
a friendship,
a relationship,
a connection from clumsy communications.
I want to lay words at your feet
like stepping stones
to lead you back to me.
I want to make these lines
into something more solid
than squiggles representing grunts
and expulsions of air
that people long ago
agreed to have some meaning.
I look at my hands and see hooves.
Without your face cupped here,
without your touch making me feel
like we were meant to touch,
what use are these things?
I want to toss these words.
I want to throw my phone
and its two,
sometimes three, bars of reception.

I want to bridge this distance
between where you are
and where you should be.
Place your hand in mine.
I promise I can be sturdy enough
to make my skeleton form
over overflowing lake
and washed away road.
I'm good at it.
Let me do something else more real
than wield these words
and give me something more satisfying
to hold and twirl between these fingers
than this bull-pen.

My birthday poem

My mouth is a cage
that holds the things I don't say to you,
the questions I don't place into your lips
just yet.

They knock against my throat
and flit in and out
of the gaps between my teeth.
The gristle has to be brushed
and flossed periodically.
I've silenced more "I love you"s
than I've spoken.
The silence is a parachute
that keeps me from plunging
9.82 meters per second into your chest.
The unspoken promise of
this.

What I've asked of you
is dwarfed by all of the things I do want.
It is my birthday
and I am not here.
My hunger,
my animal rage,
my ache to belong,
threatens to pull me right there.

I stand over your body
with a blank journal in my hands
filling pages and tossing them
at your feet.

Giving some voice
to the captive confessions
I wall away from you.

I made this for you.

And this.

And this.

And this.

And this...

Untitled

And I turn something ugly
into something that at least
feels beautiful.
The cauldrons of mouths
made to hold onto secrets and fears
and recipes for disaster.
It is a magic that is mine.
I know it well.
I feel it in the mindless movement
of my tongue hitting the roof of my mouth.
In searching for something better.
Words that don't feel like I have to question
their origin or meaning.
I don't want to think.
I just want to create.

Of altered altars

You are the remnants of a society
that escaped our records.
A people who had no need to commit their chronicles
to an unfathomable forever
when they had the intimacy of tongues
and whispers at their disposal.
When they had the urgency of here,
now,
precious,
and fleeting.

You are the offering to deities
whose names may as well translate to "I."
You are the food and the altar.
You are the clumsy lamb and the immaculate marble.
You are the sacrifice and
the rebirth from that sacrifice.
My mouth is split between
digging out hallowed hollows
into your flesh
and saying your name to conjure you with me
for as long as the pillars can bear the weight
of my desires.
I cannot do both.
Believe me,
I've clearly tried.

I don't apologize that my unlearned worship
is messy and fanatic.
I don't second guess the call I feel
in the anticipation-filled gaps of my breaths,
to press myself into you.
I am only doing what others have done

with desperation pouring out of pores.
I am watering the crops.
I am searching for the recipes,
for miracles that fit in my arms.
I am calling to the heavens
for a bountiful harvest
of bread and wine and meat.

Remember even when you forget

This crazy life will make you forget yourself,
will vanish portions of who you are
into the corners of rooms
that you have to compartmentalize away,
lest you scream into traffic,
lest you can't recognize
where the pieces go
to rebuild who you wanted to be
before.

Remember this:

You love the feeling of the air on your face
as the traffic pushes you faster
than 2021 Charles ever felt comfortable driving.

Remember that you love singing
despite having no actual ability to carry
anything resembling a tune.

Remember that you love knowing
that every single step you take
is a step your ancestors dreamed about.
How painfully beautiful is that truth?

Remember that you love words.
The way they pour out
like it's the easiest
most important thing
you have ever done.

Remember that your grandma taught you.
Your mom taught you.
Your wife taught you.
The perpetual truth
that this moment
is always sacred.

Remember.
You will forget.
You will drop these crumbs in the gaps
between today and tomorrow.
In the time between direct deposits
and another month paid for.
That's okay.
Always, remember
to remember.

I am not responsible for what I write at 3 a.m.

On accidental smoke rings
that float away like whispers.
On random women
whose freckles form constellations
I name and turn into folklore.
On shooting glances
and on happenstance.
On answers to questions unasked
and on coin flips in bad weather.
On the color of the sky
before the sun is visible
but its light is ushering it
into the horizon.
On full and new moons
and on full and new appetites.
I wish...
I could stop thinking about her.

Man of mirrors

Gena calls me a "man of mirrors."
That I reflect back what is given to me,
taking it in and changing it
before rebounding it back out.
Both mine and not mine.
Both theirs and not theirs.

The image has been off for a while now.
I have had to be my own mirror and my own light.
Away from the sound of my name
carried across downtown traffic
or in a bar or café bursting with poets.
Removed from the way my people used to feel
along the width of my shoulders,
pressed against my chest in embraces
that weathered my ribs into smooth framework.

The waters are very still here
(until they are very much not).
Every surface of river or lake
is a glassy mirror that does
what I've accidentally done before.
Make shiny warped things
of sky and sun and face and smile.
Like staring deep into the eyes of a lover
and feeling consumed by the sight
of myself wholly absorbed and loved and seen.

I've had to sit in the quiet
with the things I want to make pretty about myself.

The discordant echoes of what I am
versus what I claim to be.
What I can be
over what I probably never will.
The harm I do not want to do
and the harm I do regardless of intention.
I have had to sit in the quiet of calm around storms.
As I throw stones
and bones
and lies
and hopes
and trace ripples
back to myself.

A polyamory break-up poem

The thing I wasn't prepared for
is not getting over departures.
I carry
"what could have been"s
like injuries
that only make their presence known
when the barometric pressure
is too high.
When I sleep wrong
or put too much weight
on the right (wrong?) knee.
Can you objectify your own romantic past?
Can you gentrify pieces
of your story that were crafted
by someone's presence
as much as their absence?

My lips are time machines.
My writing is a way
to clone my finite heart.
My favorite spot
on my own body
is a place where others used to
play and live and work and dream.
My poetry is me realizing
I've been saying the same thing about myself
for almost 2 decades.
I just know better words.
And I'm not trying to make everything rhyme anymore.

–

What I wasn't prepared for
was seeing my mouth morph
into a cemetery.
Each tooth etched with a different name,
the date I first said "I love you,"
and the date I stopped.
I kiss another mouth
and glance down
to see if I've dragged
dirt or flowers or blood
onto another alter.
You learn to feel the difference
in inflection.
In tone and the shift of eyes.

"I love you."
(You are a work of art I wish I could study)

"I love you."
(I want to lock you in my sternum
and show everyone
my second heart)

"I love you."
(I made this for you.
I won't know how to stop making these for you
for a long time)

"I love you."
(Every laugh you ever gave me
is nestled in my pores).

–

What I wasn't prepared for,
the question of what to do
with the other half of the treaty.
The boxes and books and lanterns
and poems and words and trenches.
This isn't ten years ago.
I don't exorcise my ghosts
with burnt offerings,
but sleepless seance.

Another after

I write and try not to make
villains of my past.
Try to quiet down the impulse
to make things dirtier,
prettier,
than they actually were.
There's gratitude in all of it.
The beginning,
the way every possibility has long arms.
The way the threads of what love can be
don't ever end.
And the lessons, yes.
The way nothing ever teaches you
like the feeling
of letting someone you saw
a thousand tomorrows with
live on as a yesterday.
But every kiss happened.
Every time I felt alive
in the narrative of another heart,
the closing of a chapter or a book,
never erases any of it.

I have loved and lived
a hundred lives.

Normal ass poem

A storm is brewing,
sitting over the city,
impartial to whatever locale
its bottom will eventually drop out over.
Right now,
my words are not metaphors
for grief or heartbreak or violence.
Right now,
the only sounds I hear
are songs that hit
in the perfect places.
Right now,
the wind is cooling
and the clouds shoo away the sun
because this is a day
for rain and not sweat.
Right now,
I am happy and fulfilled
and grateful
to write this normal ass poem
on this normal ass day.

I'll probably end up dying in Thailand

Sometimes, I forget how far south I am.
Logically, I get it.
I drive to work and the mile markers tell me
that I am closer to the Everglades
than I am most other places.
I can open Google Maps and visually comprehend.
My two fingers making a compass along my phone,
holding hundreds of miles in my hands,
folding Florida back against itself.
I would smash into 30A.
But then, the season of hurricanes gets here.
And I remember that I am a barrier reef
against the slow churning violence
borne off the coast of Africa.
Devan doesn't want us to die here.
Doesn't want our calcium to be lost
to the sands as cities are gradually built
more inland.
But something about it feels
like a really good story.

4 River Ways (after Jamey Jones)

1) I count the rivers that usher my return
to my new home
after coming back from my old.
1-2-3-4.
Like a child's game.
Like the names of streets
on quiet nights of pitch
through which I traveled home from work
when I didn't have a reliable car.
Hood.
Ensley.
Johnson.
Burgess.
Landmarks to make the trek
feel less long and less lonely.
The stretch of pavement
between the place where hundreds know me
and the place only a few do.
It is an isolating spectrum to travel along.
The middle,
like in most parts of my life,
is my enemy.
Now,
when I pass Tampa,
I know that I am almost
back to where I belong.
The highways broken up by palm trees,
the geometry of waters pushing through the spectrum.
Manatee.
Myakka.
Peace.
Caloosahatchee.

2) This land is so flat.
Not gifted with the topography
of Alabama or Georgia
bleeding over across the borders,
the next exit,
the next stage,
feels blocked away
by my lack of vision.
It's a lesson in object impermanence.
The waters help me remember
that I'm still bound to it all.
That I'm not forgetting portions
back in Pensacola,
lost among my neice's toys
or losing layers of myself
as the wind whips past my left arm.
I am every bit of who I am
even if I can't see past some vanishing point.
Still brother and son.
Still writer and wanderer.
Still friend and fool.
Still a living memory encased
in the love I'm never fully sure
I'm totally worthy of.

3) I never have enough time
or cargo room
to carry it all with me.
I can't pack up the sound
of the Saenger Theatre erupting in applause
all around me and my words.
I can't tow the feeling
of my heart nearly bursting
with the indescribable ache of family
every single time I am with

Brian, Hannah, and Scarlett.
Not in a way that actually has weight,
is measurable,
is something I can point to
and show the streets of Lee and Collier,
this,
this is who I am.
Let me lay them strewn down I-75.
Let me show the alligators and the mangroves,
the Haitian migrants and indigenous communities,
the shine of wetness at the corners,
the pleasant violence
of accidentally re-defining myself a dozen times,
the anarchy of a collection
of punks and misfits and hypocrites.

4) I can't do the reverse either.
I cannot scoop up every sunset
that I've seen down here
burn itself into destruction
against the seemingly endless gap of the gulf.
I can't bottle the constellations
written in the sky by lightning
raking across miles.
I can't pack away
all the discordant lessons I've learned
in neat boxes and pretend
they didn't almost end me.
But I am here.
I am home,
mindlessly losing track of the time
when I wasn't.
1-2-3-4.
Manatee.

Myakka.
Peace.
Caloosahatchee.
The sun drinks up
the remnants of storms along streets
that gave me my name.
The clouds,
softer than dreams,
hold on to liquid that has touched
damn near everyone I have ever loved.
I turn on the faucet in my kitchen.
The well beneath my home
is a portal,
is a wishing fountain,
is a pipe that pours out
4 rivers
and 2 homes.

WHERE I'VE LAID MY HEAD

Notes & Acknowledgments

-The title for the poem "The bridge is over" comes from the song of the same name by Boogie Down Productions and is about my mother, Rose Moorer. I come from strong, faithful, courageous women. I have so much pride in that. I love you mom. Thank you for giving me this love of words. You began all of this and I can't thank you enough.

-The poems "What will I do?", "Six years" and "Days like these" are about my grandma, Lelia Williams. She was born in 1913 and died in 2013. She is the reason I believe in anything. This and everything that comes after is for her.

-The poem "Busy Bee Mercantile" is for Marni and the title comes from the grocery store that she opened next to the apothecary she also owned and ran for years. It was an absolute honor to read this at the grand opening and offer some small blessing in return for all that she has given the community of Pensacola, FL

-The poem "Return to Sender: A request for my next life" is for my friend, Christopher "Scott" Satterwhite. You are a fucking treasure. Please let me know if you use this book for your class. "Oh yeah, some college kids are being taught my poetry" is probably the coolest thing I can ever say.

-The poems "The world will become too environmentally and economically unstable to sustain life so I refuse to have children: A love story" and "I want to sin in ways that bring down cities: an erotic novella" were first published in this form in a self-published chapbook I release in 2020 titled *On a Random Bookcase in My Mind.* And these two, along with several others in this collection, are about my wife Marissa. Marissa, I love you from parts of myself that science will never discover or name.

-The poem "Code-switching 'for the devil catches us" was first published in *Love your Rebellion Issue 17: Riot 2022.* Thank you Angela for giving a Northwest Florida poet his first taste of Southwest Florida.

-The poem "Estd. 1898" is dedicated to any theoretical time traveler of color and to the weird fascination for nostalgia for a past that wasn't kind to many of us.

-The poem "If these bricks could breathe" was first published in *Hurricane Review*, by Pensacola State College 2021. It is written in honor of John Sunday, an amazing icon in my hometown of Pensacola, FL. Learning about his life and writing this poem changed me forever. In 2022, I performed this poem at The Saengaer Theatre in Pensacola while the beautifully talented Pensacola Symphony Orchestra performed George Walker's "Lyric for Strings." Go back to that poem and read it again while listening. And think of John Sunday.

-The poem "Katie Garrett and Mike Ensley are still garbage people: A goodbye letter to Pensacola" is, as the title suggests, about leaving Pensacola. Pensacola is a naval gulf coast town in Florida, hugging the border of Alabama. It is the first thing many see when entering the state and the last many see when leaving. It was my home for 33 years of my life. I raged and rallied. I learned and taught. I fell in love and healed heartbreaks. I was in the middle of a community of poets and punks and anarchists and geeks and some of the best people I know. Other than two exceptions, this poem and this book is for Pensacola.

-The poem "Anam Cara" gets its title from the Celtic idea of "soul friend." Thank you, Gena.

-The poem "A polyamory break-up poem" is for Robin, Emily, and Alex. In the space of a year, I found, fumbled, and lost love three times. Thank you all for the space in your hearts and lives. For every kiss and all of the love.

-The poem "4 River Ways (after Jamey Jones)" was inspired by my friend Jamey. The poet I shared a symphony stage with. The former Poet Laureate of Northwest Florida who believed in me so much, he thought I could have taken his place. I admire you deeply and your belief in me is more humbling than my novice words can convey right now.

-My forever friend Amy and the way no amount of time or distance can feel like it really interrupts us.

-Kreed and Jen and every step we've taken from dumb kids to dumb-ish adults.

-Brian and Hannah and Scarlett, my heart nearly bursts when I am around you. Compound for life. Always.

-To my Poetry Family. All of you. It would take too long to list every name that I've shared a mic/stage with. But please know that I wouldn't be the poet I am without Tuesdays and a couple hundred of the best artists I have ever known.

-To every face who has offered me a smile and love when I needed it the most. To the flora and fauna for giving me peace. To every clap of hands and every rainy day preceding and succeeding a hurricane. To every river I've walked alongside. To every tree I've touched and dreamed and loved under. To every heart I have loved and will ever love. To every sleepless night when I thirsted for insomnia's chaos to match my mind's own. To every friendship reconciled and healed. Thank you for giving me a safe place to lay my head.

-Thank you Flor Ana and Indie Earth Publishing. I am so grateful to have this be my first book that isn't self-published. I am grateful for the community and care that is all throughout this process and this company.

-To every single one of you who is reading this right now, thank you. Purchased or borrowed, you have become part of a dream I had when I was a kid. To get my words out into your hands. Thank you for being the culmination of that kid's dreaming.

About the Author

© Kristina Wright

Charles McCaskill is a native of Florida, born in Pensacola before settling recently in Fort Myers. He believes in his poetry being a direct reflection of who he is: a polyamorous Black man, a finalist for Poet Laureate of Northwest Florida, a political agitator, and a mourning grandson. His work explores themes of Black perseverance and joy, intimate grief, the beauty of nature, the plurality of love, and the way this gorgeous and flawed state still feels like home. *Where I've Laid My Head* is McCaskill's debut poetry collection.

Connect with Charles on Instagram:
@charlesmccaskill

About the Author

About the Publisher

Indie Earth Publishing is an author-first, independent co-publishing company based in Miami, FL. A publisher for writers founded by a writer, Indie Earth offers the support and technical assistance of traditional publishing to writers without asking them to compromise their creative freedom. Each Indie Earth Author is a part of an inspired and creative community that only keeps growing.

www.indieearthbooks.com

For inquiries, please email:
indieearthpublishinghouse@gmail.com

Instagram: @indieearthbooks